In the Book Nook

Written by Isabel Thomas

Illustrated by Natalia Moore

We took all the books and set up a book nook.

lots of books

bricks and wood

bright light

room to sit

In the book nook, I can zoom
to the Moon.

In the book nook, I can speed on a broom!

In the book nook, I can visit the zoo.

Lend me that book,
and I can visit too!

In the book nook, I might float in a boat.

In the book nook, I might chat with a goat.

In the book nook, I hug all my sheep.

n the book nook, I drop off to sleep!

Talk about the book

Ask your child these questions:

1 Where can you zoom to from the book nook?

2 What can you float in?

3 Which animal can you hug?

4 Why do you think you need bright light in the book nook?

5 Do you like visiting the library or bookshops?
Why, or why not?

6 What would you read in your own book nook?